Waldo, Tell Me About Me

 **Series**

Published by The Regina Press, Melville, New York 11747

ISBN 088271 468 6

Printed in Belgium

Waldo, Tell Me About Me

by Hans Wilhelm

Regina Press
New York

One evening, just before bed time,
Michael and his best friend, Waldo,
went outside to look at the stars.

It was a clear night and stars twinkled brightly. The two friends sat together, enjoying the beauty of the night sky. As Michael looked into the star-filled sky, he said, "The world is so big and I am so small." Then he whispered, "Who am I, Waldo? Tell me about me."

Waldo thought for a moment and said, "You are Michael. You are my friend. You are a little boy. But most important, you are God's child."

Michael looked surprised. "But I'm my mother's and father's child," he said.

"Of course you are," answered Waldo. "But God made everything and everybody, so He is everyone's Father."

With this, he lifted Michael onto his shoulders and walked back toward the house.

"You see, Michael, long before you were born to your parents, your Father God knew you and loved you. He created you for His Kingdom. You were just like an angel, made out of love, like God Himself. You were a beautiful soul," said Waldo as he helped Michael off with his shirt.

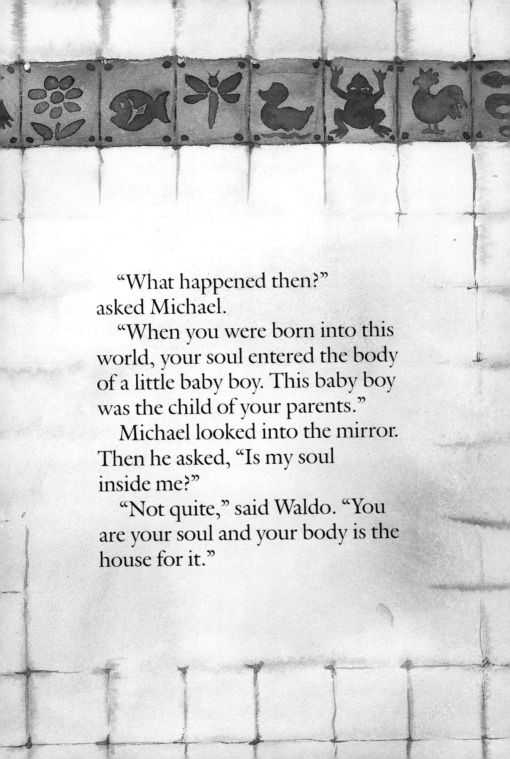

"What happened then?" asked Michael.

"When you were born into this world, your soul entered the body of a little baby boy. This baby boy was the child of your parents."

Michael looked into the mirror. Then he asked, "Is my soul inside me?"

"Not quite," said Waldo. "You are your soul and your body is the house for it."

Michael was puzzled. He wasn't
sure that he really understood
about his soul.

He needed to think about it. He looked at his toy cars and then he looked up at Waldo. "Is it like driving a car? I mean, my soul is the driver and my body is the car?"

"Right!" laughed Waldo.

Waldo watched Michael play with his cars.
"You know what happens to your cars when
you don't drive them carefully, don't you?"
"An accident," said Michael.

"Yes," said Waldo. "And if you don't take care of yourself, you can get hurt, too."

Michael climbed up onto Waldo's lap. "Does God still love me when I have accidents…or if I make mistakes?"

"Of course. God loves you so much that He wants to take you into His arms again," replied Waldo as he hugged Michael tenderly. Then he said, "Even when you are bad, God always loves you."

"That's nice," said Michael. "I like that."

"How can I find God?"
asked Michael.

"By loving," replied Waldo.

"I do love!" cried Michael. "I love
Mom and Dad. I love you. I love
my teddy."

"That's a good start," answered
Waldo. "But you can do more. You
can love everyone."

"Even Tim who throws sand in my
face?" asked Michael.

"Even Tim," answered Waldo. "When you love people who are hard to love, you get very close to God and become closer to His Kingdom of Love."

"God wants us all to find Him, doesn't He?" asked Michael as he propped Teddy up on his pillow.

"Yes, Michael. God wants everyone to be a part of His Kingdom."

"Does everyone know about God's Kingdom?"

"No," replied Waldo as he pulled up the covers. "But as we love them, they will learn about this wonderful secret."

"What will happen then?" asked Michael.

Waldo smiled. "Then everyone will find God and live with Him again."

"Everyone?"

"Yes, Michael. You, and your parents and your friends."

"Good," said Michael as he hugged his friend. "I wouldn't want to be without you."

"Neither would I," smiled Waldo. "Enough talk now. Time to go to sleep. Sunshine dreams, Michael."

"Good night Waldo."

"Good night," answered Waldo as he settled near the foot of Michael's bed.

As Michael drifted into sleep, he
whispered, "I am God's child.
That is who I am."
He hoped that he would dream
about God and His wonderful
Kingdom of Love.
And, he did.